ABOUT THE AUTHOR

Sylvia Elaine Garner was born on September 10, 1966 in NY, NY. Sylvia was born to Gus Osborne and Mella Grimsley Osborne, now Mella Grimsley Miles. Her parents divorced early on and she and her sister Sonja Osborne-Foster were raised by a single mother. Sylvia grew up in Maywood, Illinois until the age of 15 when the family moved to California due to the death of her loving stepfather, Ferry B. Hogan. Sylvia's fondest memories of growing up were mostly attributed her families road trips (Alabama, Florida, Missouri, Wisconsin Dells, WI and Canada). The most memorable moments of her teen years were attributed to Susan Miller Dorsey High School, where she was a cheerleader. Sylvia married Lindsey Garner on June 20, 1992. That union brought about two sons, Nigel and Nicholas Garner and an elder son, Jamar Garner from Lindsey's prior marriage. They reside in Palmdale, CA where they are the youth ministers at Living Stone Cathedral of Worship in Little Rock, CA, under the leadership of Bishop Henry Hearns, Sr.

Thank you to "My Village"

I thank **God** for giving me enough rope to tangle myself, but not hang myself.

I thank my mother, **Mella Grimsley Miles**, for lifting me up through the good, the bad, and the ugly. Thank you mom for taking care of you, long enough to see me change.

I thank my sister, **Sonja Foster**, for being the best big sister and teaching me what it means to be a woman.

I thank **my children** for the healing power they have to change my crazy days into peaceful ones.

I thank **Dianthea Simon** for believing in PURE and giving us our first donation ($100.00). I will never forget that!!!

I thank **LaKeisha Johnson** and **Gregory Lucky** my spiritual advisers whose jobs were definitely not easy! LOL

I thank **Staci Westbrook-Weissberg** for pushing me from day one to be the best I could be!

I thank my sistah **Lisa Nichols** for showing me and the world we can do it....No Matter What!

I thank my Business Consultant, **Dr. Octavia Brown, PhD** for helping me see and believe dreams and visions really do come true.

I thank **Traneka Hazelitt** for being the most sincere, loving and giving sistah I have ever met!

I thank **Trenita Ward** for being my mentor. She showed so many of us the only way to make it happen; was to make it happen!

I thank my Personal Assistant, **Alysa (Aly) Parsons**, for being everything I need you to be, when I need you to be it.

I thank God for my Business Manager, **Tamico Brown-Simmons**, who is my sistah in Christ and my rock.

I thank **Pastor Thomas Carter**, who is by far the realest, coolest, most down to earth man of God I have EVER MET! You are the earthly Arch Angel Michael to our family!

I thank **Elder Rodney Rivers** for your love, support and for being an awesome blessing to the LSCW Youth Department.

I thank **Bishop Henry Hearns, Sr.** for being such a legacy builder and inspiring his congregation through his truths. I have been blessed and honored to have a Bishop who cares about the youth and is adamant about building this Joshua Generation.

I thank **Laura Segura** and the **National Teen Leadership Program (NTLP)** for every opportunity you provided PURE to speak. I am also thankful for the difference you make in the life of today's teens.

I thank **Scott Manley** for the shoulder you always gave me to cry on and the hand to lift me up.

I thank **Heather Avila** for being "The One!" Only you Heather!! 4ever a friend!

I thank **my ancestors**. They were the builders of the bridges that I had to cross. They were the constant reminders that we may not always be where we want to be, but we have to make the best of where we are until better comes along. They were the wind that whispered in my ear, "we did it and so can you."

Last, but definitely not least, I thank **my husband**, the light of my life. **Lindsey**, you have seen me through all the storms, the rain and the sunshine. There's a song that says, "Can't nobody do me like Jesus." Well, you are awfully close babe! I love you more than you will ever know!!!

INTRODUCTION

I was in a horrible crash many years back. My vehicle almost totaled and I didn't have insurance for repairs. The thing that hurt the most, was knowing, it was all my fault. To be in a place where you, without a shadow of a doubt, know you could have avoided the collision if ONLY you had paid attention to the signs right in front of your face. You then begin to hear all the voices that spoke to you previously and you realize, "if I had only listened to the voices, I could have saved myself from devastation."

Well, the crash depicts my life. The insurance depicts my lack of self-confidence and the almost totaled vehicle, well that was my vessel; my body.

The signs are something we see daily, but never embrace as spurts of wisdom. They are simple, yet useful to the very core of our being. In this book, I will share seven of those signs with you and show you how they can be used to change your life, in the very least enhance it.

Proverbs 12:1 NIV
"Whoever loves discipline loves knowledge, but whoever hates correction is stupid."

YIELD SIGN

Yield signs alert the driver to any upcoming hazards or road conditions that do not reflect an IMMEDIATE condition.

In life, this sign means you need to slow down and look for things coming your way.

Parents, most times, are great indicators of when to yield. We have been down the road our teens are on in most cases. Some parents are able to drive the road with their eyes closed. It is very important to build a trustworthy parent/child relationship, so when a parent says, "I need you to yield," the teen will hear slow down. The parent wants the teen to slow down and LOOK for what may be coming.

OUR GIRLS

Teen girls-Most relational breakdowns come in the form of boys. During this time, parents begin to feel a loss of parental control because it becomes a game of tug of war between the parents and the boys; with the teen girls as the rope being pulled in different directions. In these situations there needs to be an accountability partner present (this will be discussed in a later chapter).

If our girls and young women could understand and embrace just three quotes, it would make life much easier. These quotes should be daily mantras.

(1) The grass is not always greener on the other side.
(2) There is nothing new under the sun.
(3) If it looks like a duck and quacks like a duck, it's a duck.

These mantras simply mean what they say. Open your eyes and your ears to whom and what is around you. People have a way of making something look better than it really is and we have to pay attention. Think of the card game, Three Card Molly.

In this game, you are the mark (person being scammed) from the very beginning. You know it looks and feels suspicious, but you want to play anyway (all three mantras are at work). Your yield sign goes up, but you ignore it believing you will have a different outcome, so you press on.

When playing this game there are normally other players you see win and lose the game. In reality, they are working with the card holder pretending to play to suck others into the game. They want you to follow the chosen card, normally the queen of hearts, all the while they are setting you up to believe you can win the game.

Eventually, you enter the game, they cheat you and you walk away realizing you should have yielded when the flag went up.

To all my girls and young women, many times this is what happens in relationships. It's time to stop being the mark in someone else's card game. It's time to value who you are and leave the games to the suckers.

Life is to be treasured. As parents we have invested minutes, hours, days and years into our children. When our children are threatened by something or someone, we attack to protect our children from feeling used, neglected or betrayed by others.

When we were teens, parents didn't always see the

danger lurking ahead; therefore we had to learn things the hard way. However, there were some teens that trusted in the voice and guidance of their parents and totally avoided difficult circumstances down the road.

OUR BOYS

Teen boys- Some of their yield signs come in the form of teen girls, but more come in the form of peer pressure (partying, drugs and alcohol).

When it came to my oldest two sons, one began drinking at an early age, while the other began using both drugs and alcohol because his crew was doing it. Their words are something like, "we're just trying to function." In reality, there is no function you can complete properly in a non-sober state of mind. They hear songs with lyrics like, "so what we get drunk. So what we don't sleep. We're just having fun. We don't care who sees. We're just hanging out. That's how it's supposed to be, living young and wild and free." This is the anthem of foolishness replacing POSITIVE AFFIRMATIONS.

Peer pressure is huge with boys because they want to belong to something or a group of some kind. Imagine a group of "popular boys" smoking cigarettes, snorting cocaine or even drinking alcohol and out of nowhere you're invited into this crew. You think to yourself, "they are popular and they get all the girls." This easily leads to the mentality of, "what they are doing isn't really that bad," so you begin to draw to it. The moment they reach out to you, the YEILD sign appears, but you begin to toy with the idea of allowing the thought to become an emotion. It's now exciting. You realize others want to hang out with you and it's a feeling you like because you are no longer alone.

LESSON LEARNED:

We must watch our thoughts because once the thought becomes an emotion; the emotion can quickly become an action. We begin to imitate others by doing what they do and saying what they say and smoking what they smoke. Initially, we feel a little uneasy, but as we persist, our YEILD sign begins to fade and the action quickly becomes a habit. Once the habit is formed it becomes something we do on a daily basis with our new found friends. The habit becomes a stronghold in our life and we soon find it can be something that we can't too easily shake loose.

Before the stronghold forms in your life, please pay attention. Respect and obey the yield signs in your life.

DEAD END

The Merriam-Webster Dictionary describes a "Dead End" as a street that ends instead of joining with another street, one way in and one way out.

A DEAD END is when you've gone as far as you can go. There is no choice but to turn around and go back.

For some, turning around may be liberating, for others it is embarrassing and shameful. Here is when you truly find out what you are made of.

MY STORY

When I was 19 I decided to marry my boyfriend. I bypassed the yield sign (he was incarcerated) because I refused to allow myself to slow down and acknowledge the fact.

Every person who loved me and knew me became a yield sign to me, my mom, my sister, my God sister and my best friend. However, I was on the path of righteousness for MY namesake. I knew what I was doing. I didn't need anyone to tell me anything!!! Have you ever been there? I call it the "Road to Damascus" mentality.

Once my husband was released from jail, we moved in with his sister. It didn't take long before he began to do little things like, get mad when another guy looked at me, always wanting to know where I was going, or snatch on me when I disagreed with him. SIGNS were everywhere, but in my ignorance and avoidance, I ran into a dead end.

The love taps quickly became full on beatings and at the end of one session I found myself in the middle of a standoff between him and the LAPD. Why didn't I yield like everyone told me? All the signs were there, but I refused to obey them. The consequence of my disobedience of the signs was being in the middle of a life and death situation. I was literally at the DEAD END.

By the grace of God, I was saved from physical death, but what came next was even harder than what I had just gone through. Being at a Dead End means sometimes when you turn around to go back, you pass all the same people on the path to your Dead End. This is where you either become liberated, ashamed, or both.

I became both. Even though no one made me feel that way, it was a battle to balance when to feel each one. I can honestly say, my family and friends never once said, "I told you so." They opened their hearts and their arms and welcomed me home.

Today, as well as back then, I am so grateful for all their love and support.

People often say, "When a person has had enough, they will quit doing what they are doing." I say, don't always wait until you've had enough, because you may find yourself in a grave.

Allow the natural function of signs to take hold in your life. Read and understand what they say to you. They were created for a reason.

My Mantra

The DECISION to move forward from a situation: I must leave what was behind, behind, and look ahead toward tomorrow. Praying continuously, my anger and my hatred shall not consume me. Not hatred of the person, but hatred of the things which were done to me. As a dog licking his vomit, so shall you return to the thing which calls you by name; until you have broken EVERY chain that links you to it. It knows you because it is familiar with you. It calls you because it knows you desire it and it desires to own you; but FREEDOM comes at a cost, for which I am more than willing to pay.

LESSON LEARNED:

You cannot look at the past and live according to what used to happen (he never hit me before). You must make a present day decision based on what's happening now (this will no longer be my life as of now). You must make the decision to move forward and then press on.

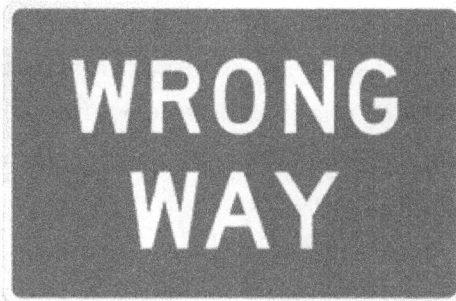

WRONG WAY

Have you ever heard the stories of drivers getting on the freeway going in the wrong direction? You pretty much know in these situations certain disaster is coming. The most interesting thing to me is when you are personally going the wrong way, more often than not; you never decrease your speed. Sometimes you go faster. Why is that?

If you're anything like me there's something in your mind telling you there is no real danger. Stay on course. What you don't realize is something has a stronghold on you. A STRONGHOLD is a demonic force coiling itself around you, suffocating the light of Jesus out of you, and telling you that you know what you're doing; when in reality you don't. I've seen it time and time again in myself, others, and even in the bible. I've nicknamed it "Road to Damascus."

In Acts Chapter 9 of the King James Bible, we are

told the story of Saul who was a Pharisee in Jerusalem who swore to kill off all the Christians. He was given the right to do this by the high priest, authorizing him to arrest any followers of Jesus in the city of Damascus.

On the "Road to Damascus," Saul was struck down by a blinding light, the light of Jesus. Saul had a reputation as a merciless persecutor of the church. In his mind, during his journey, he believed he was doing the right thing. He felt he was on the road of righteousness while he was really on the "Road to Damascus." No one could tell him what he was doing was wrong. In street talk, "you couldn't tell him nothing." Although he thought he was doing the right thing, in reality, he was going, "the Wrong Way."

When you are in this mindset, on the "Road to Damascus" it is extremely important to have an "accountability partner."

An ACCOUNTABILITY PARTNER is a person you can trust and believe in to mirror your situation back to you. At times, they will tell you something to knock you off your horse and blind you with the light of reality until you can see again.

It is definitely possible to have different accountability partners for different aspects of your life. For example, if you have someone who is good with money, they can be your accountability partner for your finances. If you have someone who is very timely, they can work with you on time management skills, etc.

You do not want to have too many accountability partners working with you at the same time because it may become overwhelming. Find an accountability partner that will start with the most important aspect of your life.

LESSON LEARNED:

If you're lucky enough to find an accountability partner to cover all aspects of your life, be grateful because it's not always easy. Remember this fact, when your accountability partner begins to do their job, they are only there to keep YOU on track and to remind YOU of the goals YOU set for YOURSELF in order to help YOU reach them.

In the end, it's really up to YOU as to whether or not YOU will be successful.

BEAR CROSSING

I bet you're thinking to yourself, "How will this fit into the story." So let's get right to it. I believe most people have seen either a documentary or a news story about a bear attacking someone. Sometimes the bear gets away, sometimes the bear is tranquilized, and other times the bear is put to death. Either way the person has been attacked and more than likely scarred for life.

In this section, the same scenario is used to describe events with close friends.

Beware of Bears

From a distance, on almost all nature shows, when you look at bears, they're big, beautiful, and cuddly. This is probably the reason most of us as children, young adults and even adults love having teddy bears. There is something comforting about being able to cuddle with them. In reality, they are nothing like they look on television. They are dangerous and extremely unpredictable. As humans, we tend to look at the outside without thinking about the inside of a person until it's too late. Below I describe a similar scenario involving my son and one of his friends.

In junior high school, my son was the kid who always wanted to make sure everyone around him was happy and having a good time. Most of his friends were girls because the boys seemed to have a problem with him. I still believe it was his Will Smith persona. I say that because he was very polite, intellectual, and always respectful to his elders and female classmates. His teacher told me he opened the door for all of the girls and pulled out their chairs.

He was very blessed with the ability to act, model, and create uplifting rap music from ages 10 to 13. During this time he went to the studio to record and everyone would say he reminded them of the young Will Smith. We were then and still are very proud of all the talents he had then, as well as his newly discovered talents.

Now, let's get back to the bear. My son had a friend he always hung out with in school whom he considered to be his very best friend. One day before school started, his best friend was told some very upsetting lies from another student that involved my son speaking negative words against the best friend's parents. Essentially, breadcrumbs were left for the bear that led directly to my son. By the time the bear approached him it was too late to do anything and he was attacked.

As children or even as adults we want to see the best in people. In this situation, we watched our son go from being a deer, wide open and free, to being a turtle never wanting to come out of his shell. My son was in an emotional place feeling he couldn't trust anyone or anything. It is a bad place to be.

The blessing in this is his best friend immediately saw the wrong in his actions. He and his mom came over to correct the situation, but that's not always the outcome. Although an apology was given, it couldn't take away the scars of the attack. We must learn to protect ourselves from bears in this world. Whether they set out to hurt us on purpose or by accident, we've learned people who are hurt in turn hurt others and it can quickly become a vicious cycle.

Lesson Learned:

When the boy and his mother came to my house all I wanted to do was hurt him so he could feel the pain he caused me when he hurt my son. I still believe his mother was more upset than I was because she insisted on handing me her child to discipline him. Her parenting skills made me respect her and in that moment I realized she was trying to raise a good child, the same as me.

During the conversation with the child and his mother, I learned he was coerced into the fight and he didn't want it to happen. The lesson we all learned that day was to open our mouths and speak to the person you have a disagreement with. Do not allow others to jeopardize your relationships.

No one wants to look or feel like a fool, but when you recognize a bear, the best thing to do is to be as silent as possible and run the opposite way (figuratively speaking).

CAUTION
AREA UNDER CONSTRUCTION

The Mindset

Three months before I met my God-given husband, I buried my fiancé. This was one of the most difficult times in my life. I was 24 years old and had just walked in from work when my sister told me my fiancé had been shot. We were two months away from our wedding.

When I arrived at the hospital James (my fiancé) mother informed me he died. His senseless death was caused by a 14-year-old boy for a gang initiation. I took a month off work and never left my house. I cried uncontrollably day and night. I wondered aimlessly, thinking about the events in my life that caused me to upset God so much that he would cause me this much pain.

This type of heartache is unexplainable. Those who have experienced it know the feeling.

James and I had been together for three years and were living together raising his three year old daughter from a prior relationship. To realize he would never be in our house or in our room again was a heavy burden on my heart. I am thankful to God he brought me through.

Three months after his death, when I least expected it, I met my husband. I wasn't looking for love and I did not want love because I was still in pain and denial about James death. A good friend of mine who worked in our high rise decided to play Cupid. Long story short, she called him, he called me, and 1 year later we were married.

This is where everyone normally begins to say, "awwwwwww," with romance in their eyes, but this is where I understood the severity of my situation. One year into the marriage, I saw the warning signs, but it was too late. I was undeniably, UNDER CONSTRUCTION.

Prior to marrying my husband, I knew I was not done dealing with the death of James. However, I thought I could handle a new relationship. I knew I loved my husband, but there this energy of anger that seemed to surround me. In June, we returned home from our honeymoon. Our family and friends welcomed us home with a trip to a restaurant to celebrate. At the restaurant, a couple of my coworkers informed me the company closed. Before departing for my honeymoon there were rumors the company may close in the month of December. However, in the week in a half of my wedding and honeymoon we received this disturbing news.

My husband took the news well, quickly reminding me of my plans to go back to school, stating it was the perfect time to do it. I decided to take him up on the offer and I obtained a degree in paralegal studies. As time went on, I began to miss James and found myself scrolling through old pictures and smelling his old shirts I kept hidden in a drawer. All along, I knew I loved my husband and this was definitely the man God had given me; but I had not paid attention to the construction zone around me and had forged ahead.

I went through the first three years of our marriage pining for someone who was no longer here. I was continually crying and going back-and-forth to the cemetery trying to understand my loneliness although I wasn't alone. In our third year of marriage I became pregnant with our son and this changed everything.

My husband was upset regarding the time I spent at the cemetery and asked me to do him the favor of never taking our son there and I agreed. I realized he wasn't asking for much and it was only fair.

After the birth of our son I began to spend less time at the cemetery and more time with our family. It was the beginning of closure for the construction zone in my life.

LESSON LEARNED:

Sometimes when you are under construction; you have to allow the work to be completed within you before you move on to your next job. In my situation, I was definitely blessed to have a man of God who was strong enough to take my hand and walk me through my deepest, darkest hours, but that's not always the case. When you are under construction, you have to take the time to complete the construction because you don't want to be on an overpass with weak beams. It may cost you not only your life, but the life of those riding with you.

STOP

Wikipedia states, a stop sign is a traffic sign to notify drivers they must stop before proceeding.

Nigel's story

Imagine having had three miscarriages and being told you will never have children. This is something no woman wants to hear. When you have faith, you know there is a plan and a purpose for everything.

I recall many days and nights, placing my hands upon my belly, telling my unborn son if he fights for his life inside of me, I would spend the rest of my life fighting for him once he came out. Who knew the power of those words would become my reality.

At age 29 I delivered my first son. He was not only the Apple of my eye, but he was the Apple. I remember prior to having him, it had been prophesied to me he would be in the hospital for three days after birth, but he would be alright. True to form that's exactly what happened. He had low blood sugar and in the end he was alright.

I'll never forget the night we brought him home. We lived in West Covina, CA. I asked my husband to participate in a ritual with me. My son was four days old and we took him outside on our balcony under the moonlight and held his naked body up to God and asked him to bless him.

As the years went on and our son began to grow, he quickly became my priority. I realize now, it was because of my prior miscarriages that he became THE MOST important factor in my life. Early on, around fourth grade, Nigel was diagnosed with attention deficit disorder (ADD). I refused to allow this diagnosis to overshadow his life and deplete him of any goals he wanted to attain. I vividly remember my niece coming home from school one day informing me of a woman who was changing lives at her school. She believed this woman could help Nigel. Her name was Selena Jackson and she was doing just that, changing lives. Selena had the knowledge of coaching people and teaching them to learn according to their learning styles. With

Selena's help we understood Nigel did not have a problem, he just learned differently.

Within one year of meeting Selena I felt our lives had been transformed into a true miracle. At the age of 10, Nigel began expressing his artistic talents including writing rap music, dancing, modeling, drawing and acting. When I think back, I recall praying for him to have one talent, but through her coaching and guidance we realized he had many.

After a couple of years pride began to rear its ugly little head. Remember, this is one of the seven deadly sins.

As time progressed with Selena, I watched my son have more fun with someone else than he had with me. It bothered me. Instead of embracing the help Selena provided, I allowed pride to come in and almost destroy a great relationship. I still pinch myself today because without Selena's guidance, we may never have realized Nigel's talents.

Nigel was always a special kid who got along well with others. When he began junior high school we clearly saw signs of depression. Due to his inability to discuss these issues, we were unable to understand his struggle. Later we realized, he had gone through severe bouts of bullying for many years and it had taken a toll on him.

When Nigel was 16, we were faced with the harsh reality of our son using drugs and alcohol to cope with the bullying and loneliness he felt. This devastated our family because we had no idea this was a concern. I spent countless days and nights crying and blaming myself and my prior sins for the troubles my son endured. The stop sign was in front of my face. Rather than placing blame, I had to find help for my son, but it took me a moment to realize I was not equipped to help him.

STRATEGY

At this point, you are faced with the question, "what do I do now?" Prayer is more essential during this time. You will have to navigate through these moments from outside yourself or your emotions will take over.

Two of my favorite prayers during this time were:
Philippians 4:7
And the peace of God, which passeth all understanding, shall keep your hearts and minds through Christ Jesus.

Exodus 14:13-14
And Moses said unto the people, Fear ye not, stand still and see the salvation of The Lord which he will shew to you today.

In Strategy mode you have to assess three things.

Where you are now?
My son is on drugs, he is stealing and he is mentally and physically killing himself.

Where do you want to go?
***I want him healthy and off drugs and alcohol. I want him to become a productive citizen in our community.
***I want him to value himself.
***I want him to face the things he has gone through and move forward with his life.

How do I get there?
***I need to find help to assist him through this troubling time.
***I need to put my pride aside regarding my fear of family, friends, and co-workers finding out
***I need to put aside my fear of not being able to do it myself. I have to be okay with reaching out to others for him to be successful.

Once the professional help has been received and the family is back on track, we must find a way to stay connected to avoid the reoccurrence of this challenge. Family collaboration is a great way to bring family closer together. Collaboration gives everyone a chance to share their opinion without anyone feeling attacked.

Collaboration is another way of saying "how can I help you move toward your goals?"

Here are a few examples of what it looks like.
***Take baby steps
***Be each other's accountability partners
***Tell your accountability partner the ways they may help you get back on track if you lose focus. This information will assist them in helping you when problems arise without warning.

We all perceive things differently for instance...

Are you working out today..." may be perceived as "oh, am I fat?"

You go shopping, hubby asks, "how much did you spend?" This question may be perceived as accusatory and then you become defensive.

LESSON LEARNED:

Be open to receiving help. Every person wants to be spoken to with respect. When you take the time to find out how your children, spouse, friends or teachers likes to be spoken to; it means that you care about them. Research their learning style and work on communicating with them in a non-combative manner. Relationships are an extremely important part of life. Make them count.

SPEED LIMIT 70

The speed limit has been set. You are allowed to go past the normal 65 MPH and you still end up doing 75 or 80 MPH and sometimes more.

What is it inside of us that drives us to push ourselves pass the limits we have been given? In some scenarios it may work for us, but in others it may work against us.

There was a time in my life when I had an opportunity to reconnect with my first love. This was the guy who gave me a promise ring during dinner at Tony's restaurant in Marina Del Rey. This was huge!! How often does that happen right? This is one of those moments in life when you have rubbed Aladdin's lamp, crossed your fingers and prayed to God for one more chance.

I know you know the prayer, "Dear God, if you could bless me with one more chance to be with them, I would do anything you ask of me." Man, we are a funny breed.

Then God grants us the desires of our heart.

Interestingly enough, I tried to relive all our high school memories. For instance, going to the movies, out to dinner, and all the other great memories we shared; but something was missing. I wasn't as happy and excited about the relationship as I thought I would be. I couldn't figure out what was different. Then I realized, it wasn't what was different, it was who. I wasn't 16 anymore and he was no longer 18. All I knew was God had given us a new start and I wasn't going to waste it.

Andre, had an amazing job with benefits and made really good money, but he sold cocaine on the side. He asked me on several occasions to try it, but my SIGNS came into play. I remembered everything my mother told me about drugs and I refused. Not too long after, I began using cocaine as a way to ignite this new found relationship. I wanted to make sure we continued to have things in common. Within one month, I had gone from a good girl who was drug free to a coke addict, snorting several grams a day (this is a lot of cocaine for those who don't know).

The observation of your speed limit is very important. Imagine you are on an open road, all is well and you're coasting at 70 mph, it feels good right? However, you want to go just a little bit faster, then a little bit more and then just a little bit more. Now you're doing 95 mph in a 70 mph zone.

Why is pushing pass the limit pertinent to our very being? It's like you have to do it. A good example of pushing the limit was during my childhood. There were several things in my house I could not touch. I never thought about touching them until my mom said, "Don't touch that." In that moment, I knew for a fact, if I didn't touch it, I would surely die (at least that was my thought). Coasting at 70 mph wasn't enough, so I chose to push the envelope.

One night in particular, I partied by myself and used so much cocaine I nearly died. If it had not been for God's mercy and grace upon my life, the spirit I saw depart from my body would not have returned. My selfishness would have caused unnecessary hurt and pain to my family and friends. I would never have had the opportunity to meet and work with the families and individuals I do today. I'm ecstatic God has shown me the purpose for my life.

I was then and still am thankful for my one and only sibling. Sonja Osborne-Foster made me take my foot off the gas pedal. She knew back then my acceleration was killing me...literally! She refused to let it happen on her watch.

LESSON LEARNED:

When you are given limitations, whether personal or professional, be sure to recognize these can lead you to a crossroad in your life. Take time to know and understand the limitations you are working with and the affect it has on both you and others. Limits are set for a reason. Knowledge simply means you know something about a particular thing or things, but wisdom teaches you to review the knowledge and push towards the best possible outcome.

Choose to seek wisdom and keep your speed within the given limit.

Purpose of this book

In my late twenties, I realized I had the opportunity to bust a U-turn and head in the right direction or continue on the road I was on. As you see my life today is much different. I chose to make a U-turn and never looked back.

Throughout my life, I have not met one person who hasn't made a mistake. The difference between me and others are the types of mistakes made and the frequency we make them.

If nothing else, I hope I've shown someone who reads this book, signs are real. Signs are powerful. Signs can be used to your advantage to create a better life for not only you, but those around you. I hope you have been blessed and encouraged by these writings.

Goals to accomplish

I want to accomplish everything I've planned on my vision board. I want to continue to not only change my life, but the lives of those around me.

I want to open a Battered Women's Shelter in Los Angeles County for women and their children. I want to ensure that they are able to obtain everything they need including food, clothing, and mental, spiritual and physical healing.

I want to be the best wife, mother, daughter, sister and friend I can be.

I want to be all that God has purposed me to be during my life here on this earth.

****

The Beginning

Who We Are:

Sylvia Garner is the President and Founder of People Understanding the Relevance of Evolving (PURE) Empowerment & Seminars. Nigel Garner is the Vice-President ad Co-Founder. Together, God has purposed them to work with individuals and families to bring them through life's storms. Their story of struggles and disappointments between parent and child has caused them to partner and change lives together for today's youth and their families.

PURE Seminars was formulated for families looking for a way to evolve out of their current crisis, create better routes of communication or enhance their overall family experience by embracing one another with love in a spirit of gentleness.

PURE Empowerment is a group formulated for the specific purpose of providing teens with the tools, skills and resources to handle life's challenges that are common amongst teens today.

Social Media Sites

Website: pureseminar.org

Twitter: @pureseminar

Instagram: @pure_empowerment

Facebook: pureempowerment

Ode to my sons

God gave me sons when man said it would never
happen
He revealed to them immediately on the ship of life
he's captain.
I'm so happy with the children you've blessed me with
this day,
I will walk in my anointing and teach them how to
pray.
If I only had them with me, one day, one week, one
year,
I would be thankful for the times we've shared each
smile, each cry, and each tear.
I humbly ask of you oh Lord to lift their burdens
today,
But if you choose not to, I'll serve you anyway.

Love Always,
Mom

www.ingramcontent.com/pod-product-compliance
Lightning Source LLC
Chambersburg PA
CBHW031531040426
42445CB00009B/480